Other WALL STREET JOURNAL. *books*

THE WALL STREET JOURNAL. *Portfolio of Business Cartoons*

THE WALL STREET JOURNAL. *Portfolio of cartoons.com*

Available from **DOW JONES** *at*
(800) 635-8349

THE WALL STREET JOURNAL.

Portfolio of Women in Business

Happy Birthday, Lily

Love,

Dad

December 24, 2000

THE WALL STREET JOURNAL.

Portfolio of Women in Business

Edited by CHARLES PRESTON

Published by

THE WALL STREET JOURNAL.

DOWJONES

ISBN 1-881944-27-1

Books can be purchased in bulk at special discounts.
For information please call (800) 635-8349, Dow Jones & Company.

The Wall Street Journal
200 Liberty Street
New York, NY 10281

Printed in the United States of America
1 2 3 4 5 6 7 8
First Edition

THE WALL STREET JOURNAL.

Portfolio of

Women in Business

"It's for the executive woman."

"*. . . and then Rapunzel bobbed her hair
and went to law school.*"

"*Arthur, don't distract Mommy,*
she's bottom feeding on the Nasdaq."

*"Ms. Appleton is our black belt
in number crunching."*

"*Are you sure you won't quit after a year or two to get married?*"

"*But Little Red Riding Hood was no fool.
She filed a sex-harrassment suit and
hauled that bad wolf right into court.*"

"*And to think all these years you've worried about some boy wonder taking over your job.*"

"... but there seems to be a
stained glass ceiling."

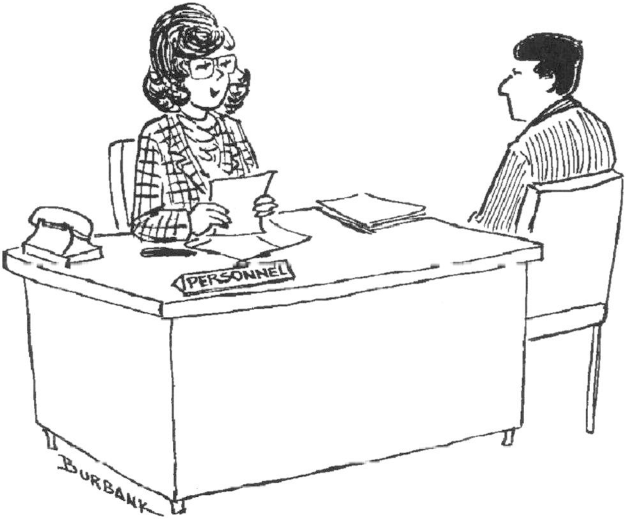
PERSONNEL
BURBANK

"Can you type?"

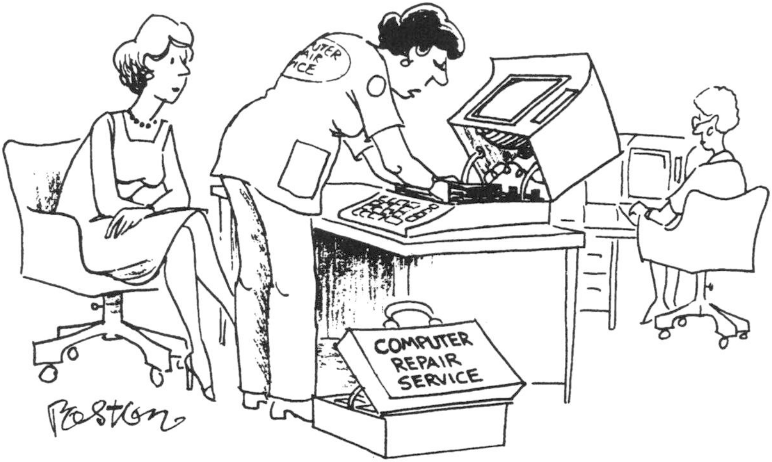
COMPUTER
REPAIR
SERVICE

"Got a bobby pin?"

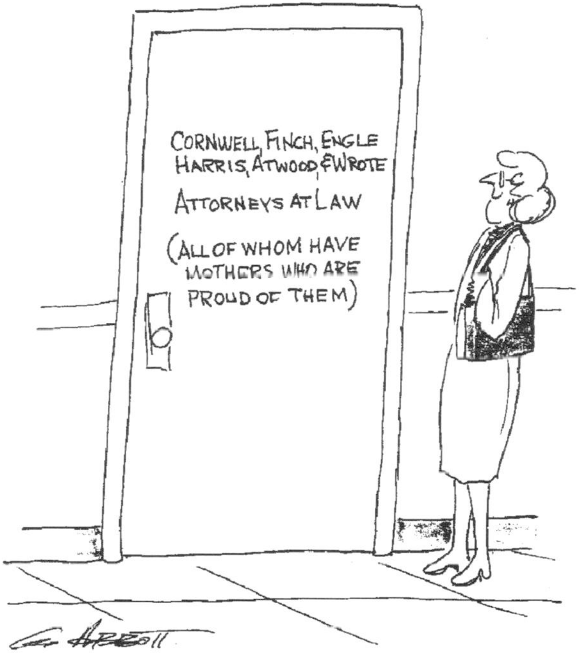
CORNWELL, FINCH, ENGLE
HARRIS, ATWOOD, & WROTE
ATTORNEYS AT LAW
(ALL OF WHOM HAVE
MOTHERS WHO ARE
PROUD OF THEM)

"*Fred, does a deflated ego count
as a workplace injury?*"

"Hello, Mom, I forgot my homework.
Would you fax it to me at school?"

"How do you know they weren't done by cavewomen?"

"I can stand the heat. I just can't
stand the kitchen."

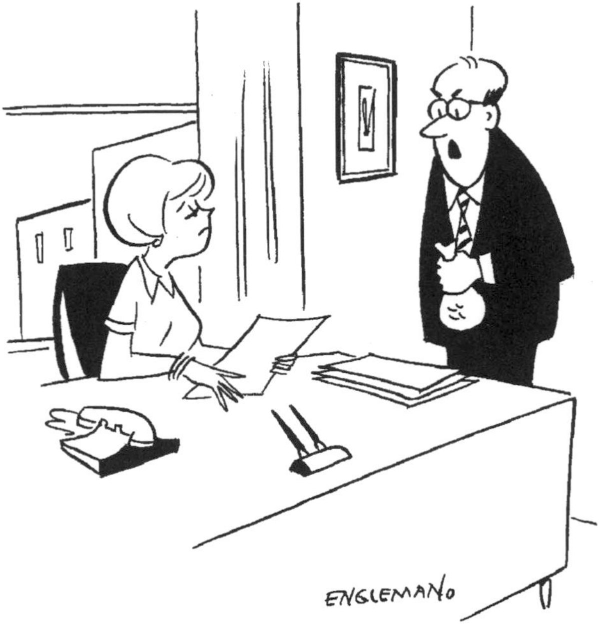
ENGLEMAN

"I don't mind working for a woman but I object to being paid in Sacajawea dollars."

"*I don't want to live happily ever after.
I want a career.*"

"*I just made enough on a stock trade to pay for lobster and champagne.*"

"*I may be a knee-jerk liberal,
but you're a knee-jerk jerk!*"

"I know you respect me Whithers,
but do you fear me?"

"*I love being a partner, Mr. Jenkins.*
There's just one problem."

"I'd like to marry you, Elaine.
Here's my résumé."

"*I said* sexist, *Mr. Marsh. Not sexiest.*"

"I'll be candid, Gwen. I find it difficult
to relate to a woman whose cigar
is bigger than mine."

"I'll take the rat race over the brat race!"

"*I'm looking for something suggestive—
of my authority.*"

*"If I asked you out to dinner, Miss Smythe,
would you sue me?"*

"I'm sorry, Bernie, but my financial planner
says you're a non-performing asset
and should be dumped."

"I've always admired the way you balance
drive and enthusiasm with good cheer.
What do you take?"

"If you make me clean my room
won't it encourage the stereotype of
the female as a subservient housemaid?"

"In between the running shoes and the dress shoes would be the running late shoes."

"In seeking a female executive to join our management team, Ms. Whitsock, we've reached unanimous agreement that you're our man."

"*Instead of learning to organize my priorities
I've become comfortable with panic.*"

*"I may look like a million, but I'm
worth much more than that."*

"It can never be, Gordon.
You're NYSE and I'm Nasdaq."

"*It was a purely professional decision, Harris. I hope my firing you won't affect our marriage in any way.*"

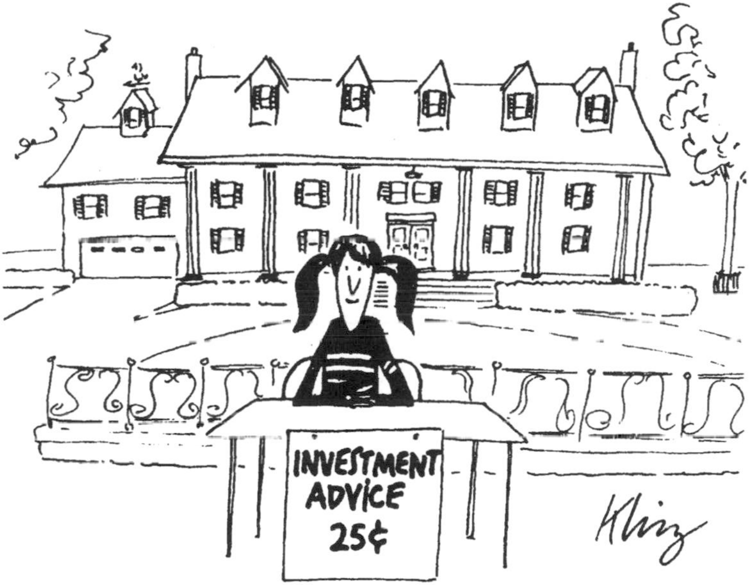
INVESTMENT
ADVICE
25¢
Kliz

"*Smedley, I think it's time we had a man-to-man talk.*"

"Marry me, Judith. . . with the understanding, of course, that past performance is not a guarantee of future results."

"*May I borrow a cup of sugar
and your software on menus?*"

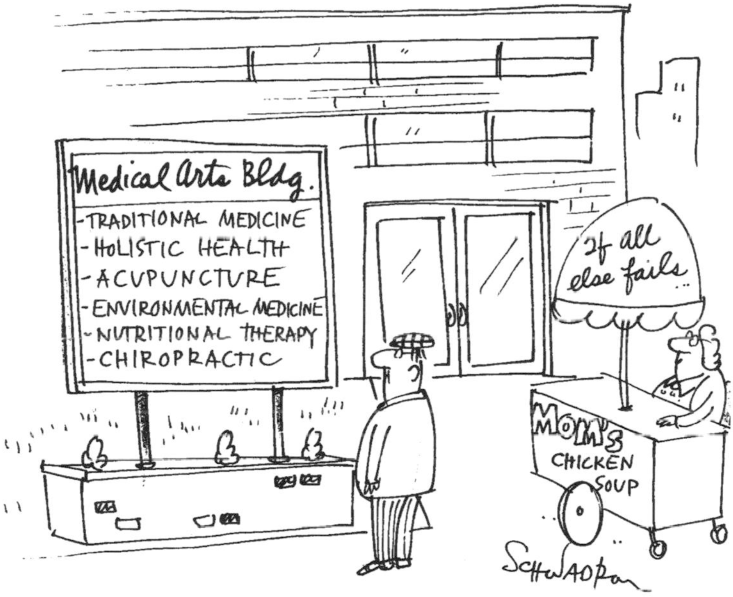
Medical Arts Bldg.
-TRADITIONAL MEDICINE
-HOLISTIC HEALTH
-ACUPUNCTURE
-ENVIRONMENTAL MEDICINE
-NUTRITIONAL THERAPY
-CHIROPRACTIC
If all else fails
MOM'S CHICKEN SOUP
SCHWADRON

"Ms. Collins heads up the progressive
wing of our old boys' network."

"*Normally I abhor tattoos, but that little one of the company logo is kind of cute.*"

"*Not now, honey, Mommy's in the zone.*"

"*Now then. . .do you want equal pay or would you rather live longer and end up with* everything?"

"Of course, the 'mirror, mirror on the wall' passage illustrates abundantly the basic insecurity of women in those times."

"*Mommy has to go out to work, because Daddy can't cut it alone.*"

"*Miss Davies, I've been looking over your file. Will you marry me?*"

"Oh, Fred's the breadwinner, but I win
the meat, the cheese, the mustard, the
vegetables, the pastries . . ."

"Oh, yeah? Wanna bet my Mommy
has more hyphens in her name
than your Mommy?"

"She's done quite well for an office temp."

"Sit down and buckle up, Mr. Weems."

"It's nice at the top of the food chain."

"*We* do *need stern financial supervision;
we've just never considered an accountrix.*"

"*Tomorrow's my wedding anniversary, Gwen.
Would you see if you can pick up
some doodad for my husband.*"

"Read me the story about Jill and
her associate going up the hill."

"Sweetie, when we leave you every day
with Agnes, we're doing it for you.
That way we can have successful careers
and you can be proud of us."

"That's my daughter, the father."

"Yes, I am a female guru.
It's taken quite a while, but I've finally
been accepted into the profession."

"You don't think it exploits men, do you?"

"*You have a Y chromosome.
I like that in a man.*"

"You know after fifteen years of high heels and ulcers, barefoot and pregnant sounds pretty good."

"*You might want to stop trying to break through that glass ceiling for a while, Ms. Gephart.*"

*"You wouldn't understand, your Honor–
it's a guy thing."*

"What the hell DO men want?"

"*Where does that leave us?*
I don't understand men and you
don't understand investment banking."

"*Where was the softer-edged, heavier Barbie during my formative years?*"

"Why do I need such a big purse?
Oh, just for 'girl stuff.' You know—cell phone,
pager, laptop, fax/modem . . ."

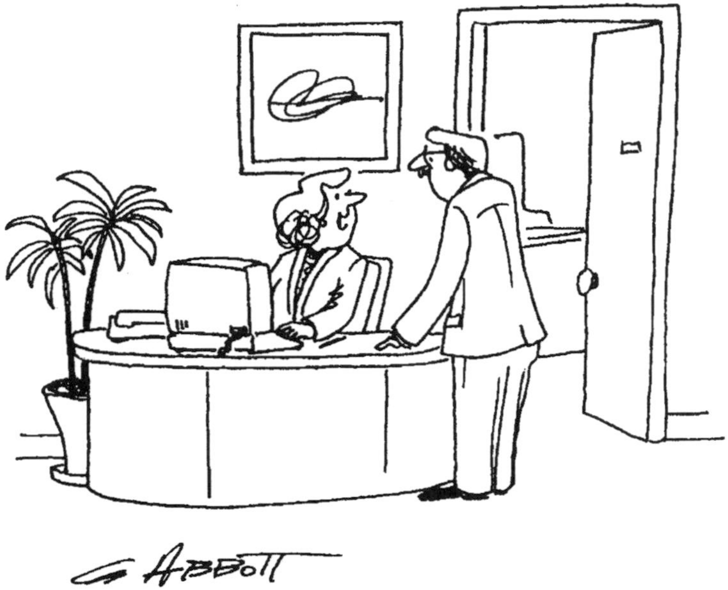
G ABBOTT

"Why I'd just love to pick up your dry cleaning. Would you like to rotate my tires?"

*"The secrets to my productivity
are clear objectives, sufficient
resources, and super-caffeinated
sugar-sweetened cola."*

"*Patience is a virtue. Please hold.*"

"Sorry, David–I'm erasing your access
code from my little black data bank."

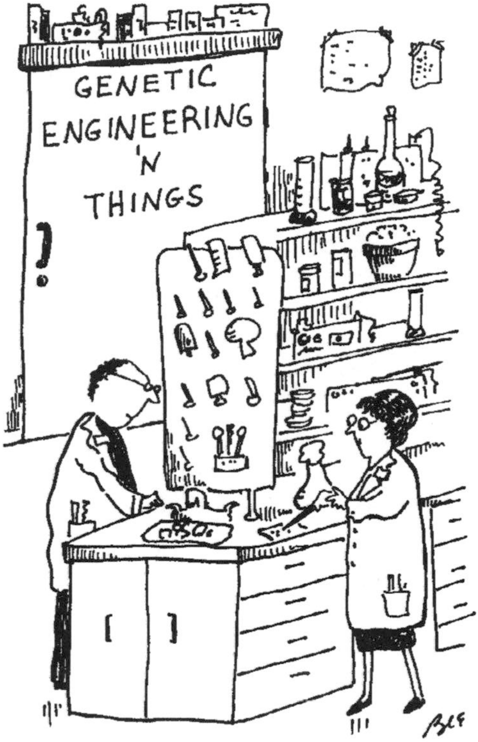
GENETIC
ENGINEERING
'N
THINGS

"I'm tired of dusting erasers, Mrs. Feeney.
Can I debug the educational software instead?"

"*I'm going to put you on hold
and I expect you to stay there!*"

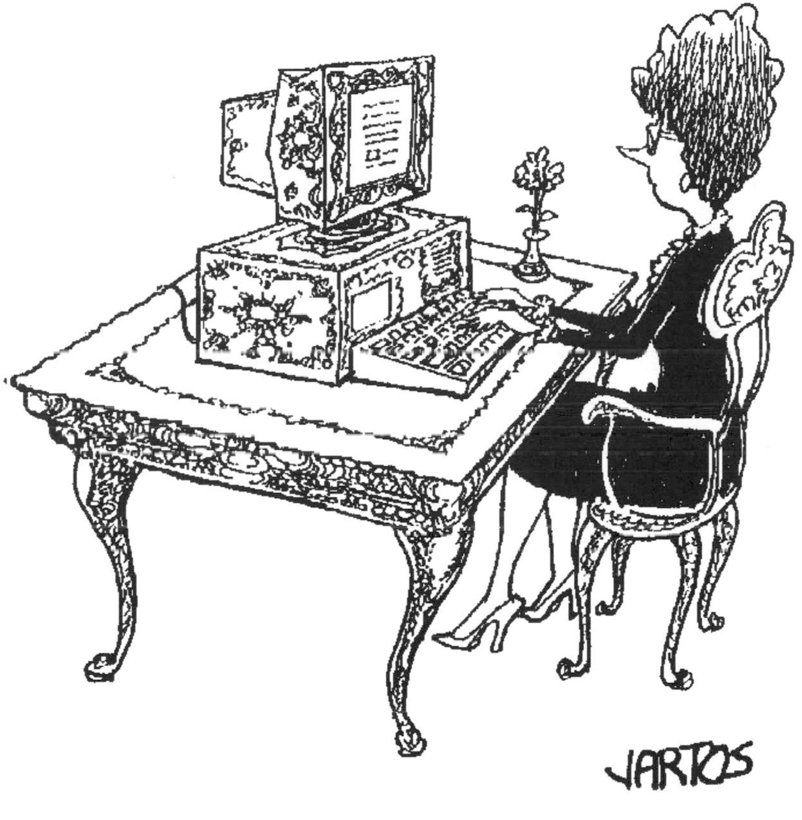
VARTOS

*"Relax. She puts on her pantyhose
one leg at a time–same as you."*

"...and so Arthur, after four years of a failing marriage, I think it would be best for us if I just move into my own apartment. Carbon copies to Dan Hayes, Chris Baldwin, and that good-looking office supplies salesman who comes in on Thursdays."

"Some day, daughter, all this will be yours."

"*You will meet a tall, dark, handsome man and you will beat him out for a promotion at the office.*"

"Uh, oh, Regina has her lawyer with her . . ."

*"When you said polished, sharp and colorful
you were describing me as your protege
not your nails, right?"*

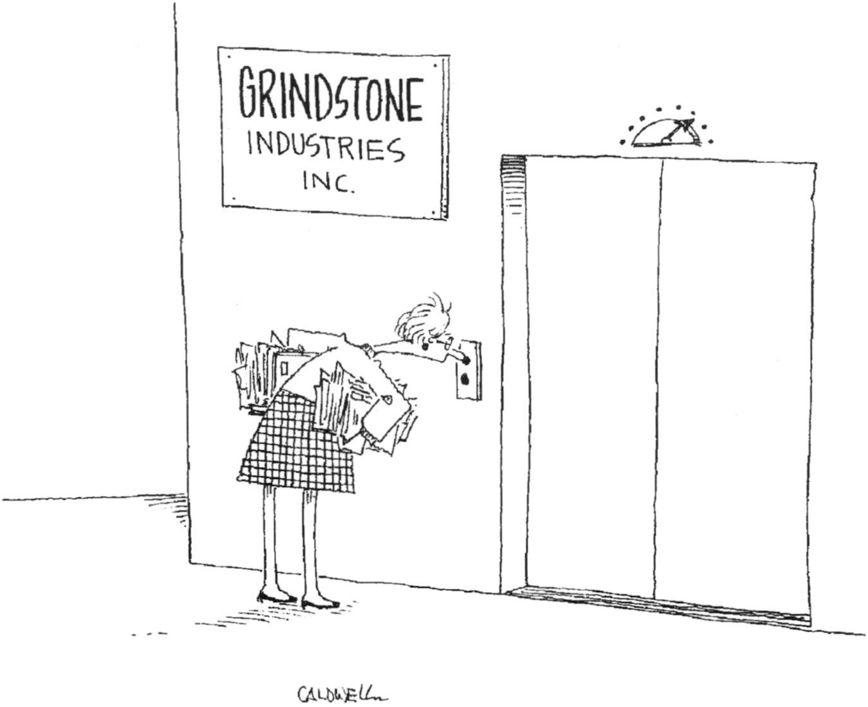
GRINDSTONE
INDUSTRIES
INC.
CALDWELL

Index of Cartoonists

George **Abbott** 11, 13, 70
Stan **Allen** 45
Charles **Almon** 24, 54

Baloo (Rex May) 2, 49, 63, 65, 75
Bo **Brown** 81
Brenda **Burbank** 9, 23, 69

John **Caldwell** 84
Dave **Carpenter** 21, 82
Thomas W. **Cheney** 3, 39
Artemus **Cole** 15, 76
Jack **Corbett** 19, 56

Nick **Downes** 51

Earl **Engleman** 16, 18
Benita **Epstein** 62, 74

Ann **Farrell** 44, 72
Joseph **Farris** 57

Randy **Glasbergen** 30, 79

Herbert **Goldberg** 80

David **Harbaugh** 40
Sidney **Harris** 61, 66
Nick **Hobart** 4, 8, 12, 35, 73

George **Jartos** 77

Mark **Litzler** 29, 31, 33, 68, 71, 83

Tom **Moran** 38

Del **Polston** 10

Thomas **Runyan** 52

Charles **Sauers** 46, 53
Clem **Scalzetti** 7, 26
Bob **Schochet** 14, 17, 25, 47, 58
Bernard **Schoenbaum** 59
H.L. **Schwadron** 1, 6, 32, 36, 41, 50,
  60, 64
Harry **Schwalb** 27
Mike **Shapiro** 42

Stewart **Slocum** 78
E.E. **Smith** 28

Mike **Twohy** 48, 67

Chuck **Vadun** 55

Chris **Wildt** 20, 43
Andy **Wyatt** 5

Bob **Zahn** 34
Tom **Zibelli** 22

Charles Preston edits the "Pepper . . . and Salt" cartoon feature, which appears daily on the editorial pages of The Wall Street Journal and WSJ.com. To subscribe, call 1-800-JOURNAL or go to http://services.wsj.com.